JOICEY ROAD SCHOOL
390 / 7000

LIVING HISTORY

THE ROMANS

Barry and Anne Steel

Illustrated by Gerry Wood

Living History

The Aztecs
Great Explorers
The Romans

The Saxons
The Tudors
The Vikings

First published in 1985 by
Wayland (Publishers) Ltd
49 Lansdowne Place, Hove,
East Sussex BN3 1HF, England

British Library Cataloguing in
Publication Data

Steel, Barry
    The Romans. – (Living history)
    1. Rome – Social life and customs
    I. Title   II. Steel, Anne
    III. Series
937   DG78

ISBN 0–85078–696–7

Phototypeset by
Kalligraphics Ltd, Redhill, Surrey
Printed in Italy by
G. Canale & C.S.p.A., Turin
Bound in the U.K. by
The Bath Press, Avon

Picture Acknowledgements:
Ronald Sheridan's Photo-Library, 5;
all other pictures by Gerry Wood.

Some of the illustrations
in this book were originally used
in *Julius Caesar and the Romans*,
in Wayland's Life and Times series.

All the words in the text which
appear in **bold** are explained in the
glossary on page 24.

Contents

How Rome began

The city of Rome stands in the
middle of Italy, near the River Tiber.
It began nearly 3,000 years ago as a
village of wooden huts, like the one below.
The Romans had a story about
how their city began –
the story of the twins Romulus and Remus.

Romulus and Remus were left to die beside
the Tiber by their mother's wicked uncle.
A she-wolf found them and fed them
on her milk, as you can see above.
When they grew up they started
their own village.
Romulus killed Remus and became king.
The village was called Rome after him.
After many years Rome became
a big city which ruled over all Italy
and many other countries.

In the city

You can see the centre of Rome opposite.
It had many beautiful buildings.
There were wonderful statues,
fountains, parks and gardens.
There were market-places and squares
where people could meet.
Below you can see an important
meeting taking place in the **Forum**.

But close by there were many dark,
narrow, filthy streets, where homes
and shops were crammed together.
Each shop sold only one kind of thing.
The streets were crowded with beggars,
pedlars and entertainers.

At home

Most Romans lived in blocks of flats.
But rich people might have a
house like the one below.
The rooms were built around a large
hall called an atrium.
The floors were covered with **mosaics**.
Houses were lit by oil lamps and candles.
They were heated by
charcoal-burning **braziers**.

Rich people ate the same kinds of fish
and meat that we do today, but they
also ate snails, dormice and peacocks.
They ate lying down,
like the people in the picture above.
Poor people could only afford fruit,
vegetables, porridge or wheat pancakes.
The Romans had no potatoes or sugar.
They used honey to make their food sweet.

A country villa

Many rich families had big
country houses called villas.
The villa was often the centre of a farm.
Most things the owner and his servants
needed were made or grown on the farm.
The farm might keep cattle, sheep,
goats, chickens and bees.
Most of the workers were **slaves**.

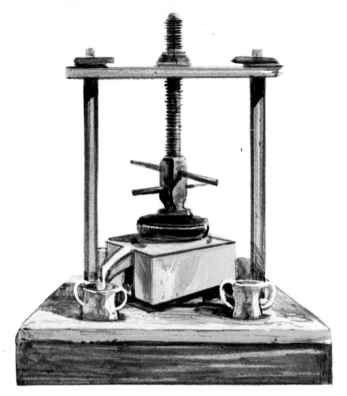

Wheat was a very important crop.
The farm would also have **olive** trees.
Olives were crushed in a big press
to make oil.
This picture shows an oil press with
olive oil dripping into pots.
The oil was used for heating and lighting.
Grapes were grown for wine.
Oil and wine were stored in large jars.

The Roman army

Rome had the best army in the world.
Roman foot-soldiers were armed with
swords, **javelins** and daggers.
A group of 80 soldiers was called a
century and the officer in charge was
called a centurion.
You can see a centurion below: he has
a wooden stick and a red-plumed helmet.

Each century had a standard.
This was a spear-shaft with badges on it.
You can see one in each picture.
In the picture above the Roman army
is attacking a city.
They are using towers to get over
the walls and a **battering ram** to
smash down the gates.

Religion

The Romans believed in many gods.
They built beautiful temples for their
gods and goddesses.
The picture below shows the temple of
Vesta, the goddess of fire.
Most families had statues in their homes
of their own household gods.
They believed these gods saved them
from robbers, illness and bad luck.

For many years, Romans were not
allowed to believe in Jesus.
But many still became **Christians**.

They had to meet in secret, because if
they were caught they were often killed.
This picture shows Christians meeting
secretly in underground **catacombs**.

Going to school

Some Roman children started school
when they were 6 or 7 years old.
Many rich children were taught at home.
The poor could not afford school.
Schools had only one teacher and
one classroom.
The school day lasted from before dawn
until the middle of the afternoon.
Here is a scene in a Roman school.

The children had no paper.
They wrote on **wax tablets** with a **stylus**.
You can see these in the picture below.
Only the teacher had books.
They were written by hand on
long rolls of paper, called **papyrus**.
Children under 11 years old learned
reading, writing and counting.

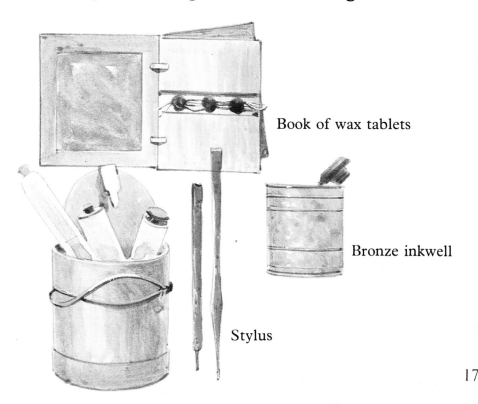

Book of wax tablets

Bronze inkwell

Stylus

Roman builders

The Romans were very good builders.
They are famous for their roads,
bridges and **aqueducts**.
Aqueducts were special bridges which
carried water instead of roads.
You can see one being built below.
Some were many kilometres long.
They brought water to the cities.

Hadrian's wall, in the north of England,
was built by the Romans to protect
themselves from the **Picts** and the **Scots**.
It is 118 kilometres (74 miles) long.
The Romans built good roads all over
Italy and the countries of their **empire**.
They built roads as straight as they could.
The work was done by slaves or soldiers.

Entertainment

Romans loved watching **chariot** racing.
Races were run in a huge **stadium**.
The winners were given a purse of gold.
The drivers had to be brave and skilful.
Chariots often crashed and
many drivers were killed.
It was an exciting and
dangerous sport.

People liked going to the public baths.
They could wash, swim or exercise there,
like the people in the picture below.
The baths were also a good place to
meet and talk.

They were beautifully decorated.
Some baths had restaurants, shops,
gardens and even libraries.

Things to do

1 A standard

You have read how each century in the
Roman army had its own standard.
Why not try and make one yourself?
Find an old broom handle.
Glue card shapes on to your broom handle.
Cardboard plates make good badges.
Now paint your standard.

2 A wax tablet

Find some thick cardboard.
Glue four narrow pieces of cardboard
around the edges of a square piece
of cardboard.
You have now made a frame.
Ask an adult to melt some old candles
and pour the wax into the frame.
When the wax has set, write on it with
a sharp stick or a nail.

Glossary

Aqueduct A bridge which can take water across a valley.

Battering ram A huge log with a metal tip shaped like a ram's head, for breaking down doors or gates.

Brazier A metal pan in which charcoal was burned.

Catacombs Underground passages and tombs.

Chariot A light, two-wheeled cart made of wood and leather.

Christians People who believe in Jesus Christ.

Empire A group of countries under one ruler.

Forum The most important public meeting place in Rome. It was also a market place.

Javelin A light spear thrown by hand.

Mosaics Patterns made on floors with small pieces of stone or tile.

Olive A small, green fruit, about the size of an acorn.

Papyrus A kind of paper made from reeds.

Pedlar Someone who travels around selling things.

Picts and Scots Two tribes of northern Britain who often attacked the Roman soldiers.

Slave Someone who belongs to another person and has to work without pay.

Stadium A large place where people watch sport.

Stylus A tool used for writing on a wax tablet. One end was sharp for writing, the other was flat for rubbing out.

Wax tablet A wooden frame filled with soft wax for writing on.

24

Books to read

A Roman Centurion by Stewart Ross (Wayland, 1985)
A Roman Town by R.J. Unstead (Hutchinson, 1977)
Living in Roman Times by J. Chisholm (Usborne, 1982)
Growing up in Ancient Rome by Amanda Purves
(Wayland, 1978)
Romans by Henry Pluckrose (Hamish Hamilton, 1981)
Roman Soldiers (Macdonald, 1972)

Index